UNICEF

FOR BEGINNERS

Written and illustrated
by Christian Clark

D0921349

Writers and Readers

unicef
United Nations Children's Fund

This book commemorates UNICEF's 50th anniversary on December 11, 1996! Part of the proceeds from sales will support projects on behalf of children the world over.

Writers and Readers Publishing, Inc.
P.O. Box 461, Village Station
New York, New York 10014

ISBN 0-86316-197-9

0 9 8 7 6 5 4 3 2 1

Manufactured in the United States of America

UNICEF
FOR BEGINNERS

This book is dedicated to Rius, the inspiration behind the 'For Beginners' series, and to Mita Hosali, long my own source of inspiration.

What goes around comes around.

I also want to thank Maggie Black and Judith Spiegelman, whose work became the basis for this project, and Catharine Way and Michelle Siegel for their creative interpretation of my scribbles.

And last but not least, thanks to Pierce Gerety and the UNICEF Somalia team for giving me the time off I needed to complete this book.

Contents

After the war

UNICEF is
the first international
organization created
solely to look after
the world's children.

Good idea!

Founded on December 11, 1946, at the very first session of
the United Nations General Assembly — by a unanimous
decision, no less — the
organization was named the
United Nations International
Children's Emergency Fund.
It's not hard to figure out
why...

UN Photo/IO47713/S. Lwin

World War II had just ended. Many regions of the world lay in ruins. Food, medicine and clothing were urgently needed everywhere, from Europe to China.

Look on the bright side. At least now we have peace.

It was in a broken Europe that UNICEF began its operations, replacing the main postwar relief agency, the UN Relief and Rehabilitation Organization. At the peak of its activities there, UNICEF provided 6 million children with daily meals and milk, earning UNICEF the nickname **"milkman to the world's children."**

A week after UNICEF was born, **Dr. LUDWIG RAJCHMAN,** from Poland, was chosen as the Chairman of its governing body, the Executive Board. This was a choice that would mark UNICEF's direction long after the postwar emergency was over.

For Dr. Rajchman believed that child nutrition and maternal care must be incorporated into routine medical practice — an idea seen at the time as, well, revolutionary.

Dr. Rajchman's insistence on self-help remained another UNICEF cornerstone.

On Dr. Rajchman's suggestion, the UN Secretary-General appointed humanitarian **MAURICE PATE** as UNICEF's first Executive Director. Remember, the war was very recently over; anger, bitterness, even revenge were still running high. Pate thus posed one condition to his candidacy: He would accept the post only if all children in need in any country, including the former Axis countries of Germany, Italy and Japan, were eligible for UNICEF's help. And so was set another UNICEF cornerstone:

CHILDREN'S NEEDS MUST BE KEPT ABOVE POLITICS.

✳ ✳ ✳ ✳ ✳ ✳ ✳

The mandate conferred on UNICEF in 1946 was deliberately broad, allowing the organization the flexibility to work wherever it saw need. The Executive Board decreed that "UNICEF works on behalf of children on the basis of need without discrimination with regard to race, creed, nationality, status or religious belief."

So tell me more about how UNICEF is run.

GLAD YOU ASKED!

Although UNICEF's activities are carried out by the Executive Director, the policies are determined by the Executive Board.

The Executive Boar?!

No No No!
The Executive Board!
Members of this Board are elected by the United Nations General Assembly.

And one more thing. (All right, two.) The Executive Director is appointed by the UN Secretary-General in consultation with the Executive Board. And, funded entirely by voluntary contributions, UNICEF always works in cooperation with governments, and at their request.

Back to the post-war emergency. . .

It wasn't just food that was in desperately short supply. So too were medicines, soap, clothing and

SHOES!

Indeed, with no shoes, many children stayed home from school, missing not only an education but that daily cup of warm milk. Some children went to school anyway; barefoot in the winter, they contracted tetanus, pneumonia and respiratory infections.

Australia and the UK, two of the largest leather producers in the world, were asked for help. As a result, 2 million pairs of shoes and boots were made and distributed to needy children.

Courtesy of the American Red Cross

Of course, it wasn't just European children who were suffering after the war. So were the children of Asia. In 1948 UNICEF began working in China. The country had had no time to recover from the global war when it was torn apart by civil war. UNICEF was able to set up feeding centers in government-held territory and provide medical equipment and technical assistance in Communist areas.

Better fed than dead!

That same year, UNICEF began working with refugee mothers and children in Palestine. Then, a year later, in 1949, UNICEF really stretched its wings, starting programs in Latin America. Indeed, within five years UNICEF would be operating in almost 100 countries and territories.

But nobody could have predicted all this. Even as it was making such strides in the late 1940s, UNICEF's future was in doubt, because the postwar emergency was receding.

That, after all, was why UNICEF had been born. Its work was supposed to have been temporary.

Now, wait one second! What about the kids all over the world who had nobody to turn to?!

GOOD POINT! Still, there were three arguments against the continuation of UNICEF:

MONEY! In 1949, the U.S. Congress, which underwrote a great deal of UNICEF's budget, thought it was time to call it quits.

TERRITORY! The UN's World Health Organization, and to a lesser extent the UN's Food and Agriculture Organization and Bureau of Social Affairs, did not appreciate the idea of a separate UN organization for children.

 MANDATE! UNICEF, if it were to move beyond post-war emergency relief, would need to think through longer-term development goals and strategies.

UNICEF's FUTURE WAS HANGING IN THE BALANCE.

1950s

On October 6, 1950, the critical debate on UNICEF's future was held at Lake Success, in New York state. It was decided that UNICEF in its existing form would be extended. But for only three years!

Still, even this was a victory. Especially since influential Eleanor Roosevelt, the chief U.S. delegate to the meeting, was not convinced of UNICEF's importance.

Oscar Berger

Yet Mrs. Roosevelt soon changed her mind: The more she got to know about UNICEF, the better she liked it.

But the question of the organization's continued existence was not finally settled until October 5, 1953. It was then that the UN General Assembly agreed that UNICEF should continue 'indefinitely'. The words 'international' and 'emergency' were dropped from its name, but UNICEF's well-known acronym was retained.

It was this debate in 1953 that made people realize that the world faced another emergency — but this one did not result from war. It was later to be named the **silent emergency** — the spiral of poverty, disease and hunger that kills thousands of children every day, especially in Asia, Africa and Latin America. UNICEF could do much to help children caught in this insidious crisis.

In fact, it was Mrs. Roosevelt herself who came to UNICEF's defense during that debate in the General Assembly. She spoke these widely quoted words...

"There are about 900 million children on earth today. More than half — about 500 million — live and die in want... They are familar with hunger, cold and disease. The only organization that even begins to answer their needs is UNICEF. Yet its total expenditure is less than half the cost of a single battleship... My hope and the only practical salvation for these children is that UNICEF will be made permanent."

But UNICEF's problems weren't quite over yet. The anti-Communist paranoia in the United States during the 1950s cast a shadow even on UNICEF, with some fervently patriotic groups blasting 'red influences' in the organization. For instance, the Daughters of the American Revolution described the character of UNICEF greeting cards — which in the early days avoided religious messages — as "a Communist-inspired plan to destroy all religious beliefs."

More serious, however, was a decision by the US Congress to subpoena UNICEF's Chairman, the innovative Dr. Rajchman, to appear before an anticommunist subcommittee. As the head of an organization largely dependent on US funds, Rajchman felt the most graceful response would simply be to step down. He lived out his retirement in France, maintaining close links with UNICEF until his death in 1965.

Throughout this time, UNICEF remained focused on children's health needs. The 1950s, from a medical perspective, were a time of tremendous optimism. 'Miracle drugs' like penicillin were being discovered. So were insecticides against such creatures as malaria-bearing mosquitoes.

You call that good news?!...

And the prices of life-saving drugs were dropping. So UNICEF, in partnership with the World Health Organization, set out to do what no one had done before: launch a **mass disease campaign** to fight the illnesses affecting millions of children

Yaws, Syphilis, Trachoma, Leprosy, Malaria, etc, etc.

In Asia, it was Sam Keeny, UNICEF's first Regional Director, who did the most to help governments tackle age-old threats to children's health.

With his public health background and political acumen, Keeny's campaign against yaws in Asia was the most impressive example of how 20th century scientific advances could be exploited in the war on disease.

He showed how to get miracle treatments to everybody, not just the rich elite.

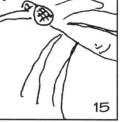

Yaws was the disease that fell earliest and most spectacularly to the mass campaigns. Yaws is a tropical disease spread by open sores that cause boils all over the body. What begins in childhood as a painful sore can become a crippling condition by adulthood. Yet the disease can be cured by a single shot of penicillin!

It's a miracle!

From 1949 through 1969, UNICEF and WHO cooperated with governments in 50 countries to eliminate yaws. About 160 million people were examined and almost 60 million treated.

UNICEF/ICEF 372

This Haitian girl's deformed lips and the sores on her elbow are a result of yaws. The disease once crippled half the Haitian population. After a nine-year UNICEF-assisted government campaign, it was virtually eliminated in that country.

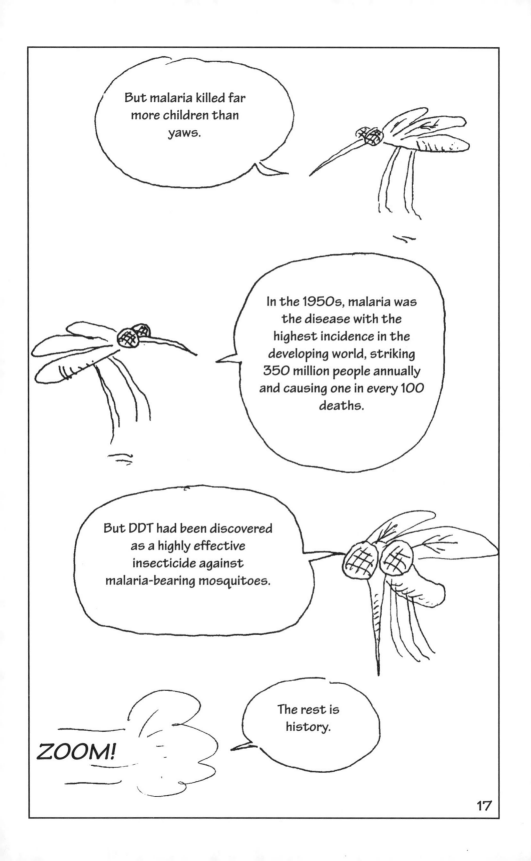

Except it wasn't. The idea of halting malaria by spraying household walls with DDT a couple of times a year sounds simple. But in practice, it meant reaching 75 million homes in India alone. By 1953, UNICEF was spending around $6 million a year on DDT to protect 13 million people — a small percentage of those afflicted — and some governments had run out of money for spraying programs.

Nor was it just a question of logistical problems and money. In some areas, mosquitoes became immune to DDT. And concerns began to grow about the health effects of DDT. Clearly not all the scientific breakthroughs of the era were as simply perfect as they first appeared. In 1959, the UNICEF Executive Board imposed a gradually declining ceiling on malaria expenditures. The dream of eradicating malaria has not yet been realized.

Score one for us mosquitoes!

But UNICEF continued its aggressive assault on other fronts.

Soon other health campaigns were launched, which tackled:

Trachoma, a painful eye disease, and once the world's leading cause of blindness. By the end of the 1950s, 6.5 million children had been treated in Asia alone.

Leprosy, the disfiguring and stigmatizing skin disease. By 1955, UNICEF was assisting eight anti-leprosy programs. An estimated one third of all leprosy victims were soon receiving treatment.

Tuberculosis, second only to malaria as a child killer in Asia. A TB vaccine had been developed, but it was difficult to use in tropical climates. It needed to stay cool to do its job. (Hey — that sounds like good advice for all of us.)

The **cold chain** did the trick. It's a series of insulated containers, from refrigerated compartments on airplanes to pumpkins packed with ice, that keep vaccines cold from the time they're made till they're used.

Can I interest you in a cool vaccine?

By the end of the 1950s, almost half of UNICEF's $25 million annual budget was committed to mass health campaigns against insects, parasites and viruses.

Increasingly, though, the campaigns were seen as only interim solutions to disease. The mass campaigns had been the most visible but not the only part of UNICEF's health work. Their days were numbered. What was needed was regular health services for all.

Especially for little ones like me!

UNICEF was working on that, too, by equipping health centers and training local staff in rural areas around the world, places where doctors rarely, if ever, came. UNICEF, in fact, was training all sorts of people for those centers: nurses, midwives, nutritional volunteers and traditional birth attendants (TBAs).

So many women in these rural areas were dying in childbirth. Sometimes it was because there was no one there to help them. But more often it was because those who did help them had no training in basic hygiene or medical practices.

Since the 1950s, over 500,000 nurses, midwives, and TBAs have been trained thanks to UNICEF stipends. UNICEF has also provided thousands of hygienic midwifery kits to them. The kits include among other things...

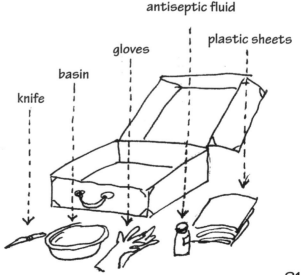

knife   basin   gloves   antiseptic fluid   plastic sheets

And where did these kits come from, you might ask? Why, from UNICEF's huge

WAREHOUSE

... And two bottles of aspirin, pronto!

The staff at UNICEF's warehouse in Copenhagen remains on emergency alert 24 hours a day, 365 days a year. When disasters strike children, UNICEF can ship relief supplies within hours.

The warehouse began operations in 1953 in the basement of the United Nations in New York. Today it ships about $100 million worth of supplies every year — 3,500 different items — to 130 countries.

To The Kids of the WORLD. Love, UNICEF xxx

VACCINES

But back to the 1950s—

During this era, milk was widely regarded as one good answer to the problem of children's hunger and malnutrition. Milk, after all, is chock full of protein, vitamins and minerals.

By 1957, 4.5 million children and pregnant and breastfeeding women were receiving UNICEF milk worldwide.

But shipping millions of tons of dried milk to developing countries was hardly a long-term solution to world hunger.

What about developing local dairy industries?

Exactly! In addition to supporting 11 dairy plants in Latin America, UNICEF helped develop a milk producers' co-op near Bombay, India, that eventually processed almost 80,000 gallons of milk a day.

Holy Cow!

Still, there were too many families who couldn't afford to buy milk for their children, even with subsidies.

So UNICEF began experimenting to find other economical, high-protein foods, such as those based on soy beans. But soon it became clear that sound nutrition, if it was really to take root, couldn't be dependent on high technology.

What was needed were simpler solutions based on the simple technologies in the villages.

Well, back to the drawing board!

It was also becoming clear that to tackle the problem of children's health and nutrition was to tackle poverty itself. And to do that effectively required taking on all its various aspects, all at once. Otherwise each separate program would find its own purposes frustrated.

This was plenty to wrestle with. But about that time something happened that made it a little easier. The UN General Assembly adopted the Declaration of the Rights of the Child.

The 1959 Declaration said, in effect, that the hunger, poverty, disease and ignorance endured by millions of children was a violation of their basic rights.

UNICEF, furthermore, was mandated to help countries carry out the aims of the Declaration. It was decided to undertake a survey to examine the situation of children worldwide.

1960s

The decade began with the Survey on the Needs of Children. It concluded that UNICEF needed to pay attention to the 'whole child', not just the child's health or nutritional needs.

This may sound obvious today, but at the time it was revolutionary!

The timing couldn't have been better, for the 1960s were soon declared **THE DECADE OF DEVELOPMENT** by both the United Nations and the new US President, John F. Kennedy.

Remember, ask not what children can do for you, ask what you can do for children ... or something like that.

With the Declaration of the Rights of the Child, UNICEF sure had its work cut out. The institution itself was undergoing a change.

In the 1950s, UNICEF had discarded its original character as a narrowly defined operation for child relief.

In the 1960s it was beginning a second metamorphosis...

...from a humanitarian and welfare organization...

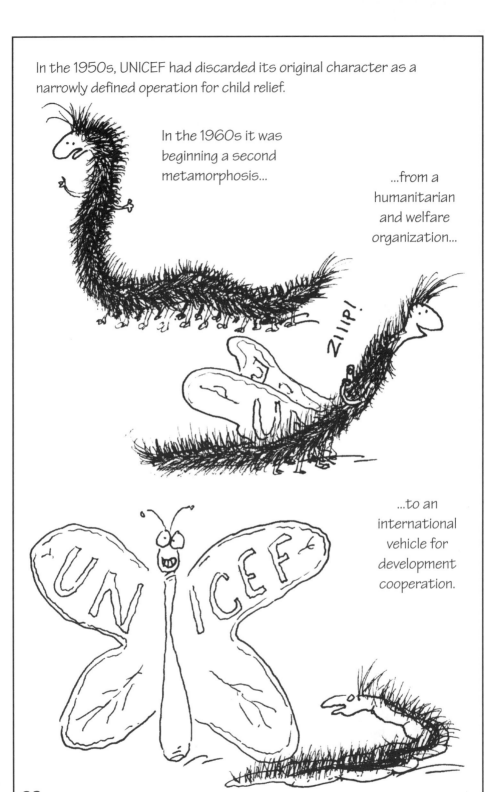

ZIIIP!

...to an international vehicle for development cooperation.

Even the old UNICEF emblem was changing. Gone was the child with a cup of milk; it was replaced by the silhouette of a healthy mother and child.

How Moooving!

The 1960s were also marked by another historical trend —
DECOLONIZATION!

PUT CHAINS HERE

The decade became a symbol of excitement and hope, as 17 African countries achieved independence and UN membership in 1960 alone. Most of the others would follow soon.

During the 1960's. the 'Development Decade', UNICEF became more bold in asserting that countries had the responsibility to take children's needs into account. The organization began to assist governments in establishing programs for children, and supported their efforts with advice, supplies and training.

Certainly one of the best ways to attack poverty and promote development is through **education**.

Executive Director Maurice Pate declared in 1960:

"It has become increasingly clear that the emphasis in future development plans will be on education."

And newly independent Africa needed educational initiatives. The literacy rate in some countries on the continent was 16 percent. Fewer than 10 percent of children attended school. There were few university graduates, technicians or scientists.

But UNICEF faced a dilemma. Despite the efforts of so many good people to fund the agency, only around $25 million was available to spend on all its programs. By 1965, schooling absorbed nearly half of UNICEF's overall assistance to Africa.

But wait a minute. How was UNICEF supposed to afford to fund its work? Where *does* the money come from, anyway?

Most of it, about two thirds, comes from **GOVERNMENTS** in the form of voluntary contributions. Individuals also contribute money to UNICEF, and many of you buy our. . .

Greeting Cards!

UNICEF has been producing those cards for a long time. And the money they raise provides funds for lots of projects.

The first UNICEF card was a picture of a maypole drawn by a seven-year-old Czech girl named Jitka who sent it to UNICEF in 1949 to say 'Thank You' for her UNICEF milk.

So many people were moved by Jitka's card that UNICEF printed it and sold copies. Within two years a full UNICEF greeting card operation was established. Some artists a little better known than Jitka got involved too: **Salvador Dalí**, *Georgia O'Keeffe* and **Pablo Picasso,** for instance.

UNICEF greeting cards are now being made by artists and craftspeople from around the world. In Nepal, for instance, greeting cards have become central to a community development project. Thousands of lives are being changed as the project revitalizes two crafts: paper-making and woodblock printing.

OK, here's an idea for a "I hope you get over colic soon" card.

Today you can buy cards for Diwali (the Indian Festival of Lights), Wesak (the Birth of Buddha), Eid Al Fitr (the Islamic Feast Day), Hanukkah (the Jewish Festival of Lights) and Rosh Hashana (Jewish New Year), as well as Christmas and New Year!

It isn't just greeting cards that have helped support the world's children.

In 1950, a minister in the US suggested to his Sunday school class a variation on the autumn celebration of Halloween, when children go door to door repeating a familar refrain: **"Trick or treat!"**

trick or treat for UNICEF

HELP THE CRUSADE AGAINST HUNGER AND DISEASE AMONG "ALL THE WORLD'S CHILDREN"

THE UNITED NATIONS CHILDREN'S FUND HELPS MILLIONS OF NEEDY CHILDREN AND MOTHERS IN MORE THAN 100 COUNTRIES

Viacom International, Inc.

Instead of asking for treats for themselves, he suggested, why not ask for nickels and dimes for UNICEF? Thanks in part to media campaigns featuring such stars as comedian **Danny Kaye** and the dog-hero **Lassie,** the idea soon caught on!

Luckily we usually get candy **and** money for UNICEF!

To date, the annual Halloween campaigns have raised more than $102 million for UNICEF.

Not to be outdone, children in other countries began raising money for UNICEF. On Julebukk, an ancient holiday celebrated in Norway 12 days before Christmas, kids dress up and go door to door singing hymns and folk songs, and asking for treats. They have raised over $1 million for UNICEF!

Similar campaigns regularly take place around certain holidays in Finland and Ireland.

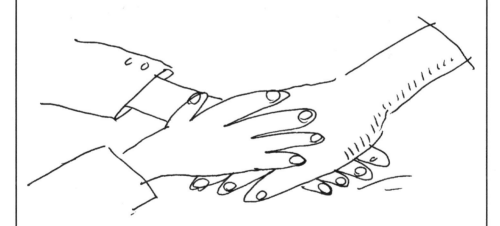

Perhaps as important as the money raised is the feeling of solidarity fostered among children of different nationalities, races, religions and economic situations — children who have never seen each other but are still able to feel for one another.

Even airlines have become involved in helping the world's children.

Since 1959, airlines have collected international travelers' foreign coins and donated the money to UNICEF. As of the end of 1995, 10 airlines* were participating in 'Change for Good'. Just since 1991, the program has collected $4.5 million for UNICEF projects.

Another group that helps raise funds and awareness for child rights is UNICEF's famous...

---

*American, Asiana, British, Canadian, Cathay Pacific, Finnair, Japan, Qantas, Swissair, Trans World

GOODWILL AMBASSADORS

In early 1950, UNICEF Executive Director Maurice Pate met comedian **Danny Kaye** on a transatlantic flight. It was a long flight and the two began to chat about UNICEF. One thing led to another. A few months later, when Kaye went to Asia, he

UNICEF/2256

took some time out to visit several UNICEF projects, with a camera crew. The end result was a film, **Assignment Children.**

It was the start of a long and close relationship. For more than 30 years Kaye served as UNICEF's Ambassador-at-Large to the world's children. Kaye was just the first of many celebrities and public figures to make appearances and raise funds for UNICEF.

UNICEF/1030/84

Saudi Arabia's Prince Talal Bin Abdul Aziz Al Saud became one of UNICEF's best-ever fund raisers, helping to bring $80 million into UNICEF coffers.

The testimony of actress **Liv Ullmann** about the African famine of the 1980s moved the US Congress and various parliaments in Europe to approve greater relief aid.

UNICEF/ICEF 8623/India

UNICEF/5103 Z/92/Press

The late **Audrey Hepburn,** who was herself a recipient of UNICEF meals in The Netherlands after the war, brought world attention to the plight of all children, from Bangladesh to Somalia.

UNICEF/ICEF 7939/Dutia

The much-beloved actor **Sir Peter Ustinov** has dressed up as a magician, a hippie, a Canadian Mountie and even Santa Claus himself for UNICEF commercials.

UNICEF/837/84/Cerni

Japanese actress and talk-show host **Tetsuko Kuroyanagi** has brought international children's issues to a Japanese audience.

UNICEF/2205/87/Isaac

Through concert performances and visits with children and government leaders, singer **Harry Belafonte** has raised both awareness and funds to support UNICEF-assisted programs throughout Africa.

And last but not least are

UNICEF's NATIONAL COMMITTEES

By 1964, National Committees had been established in 17 European nations alone. By the end of the decade, Australia, Israel, Japan, and New Zealand would have their committees as well.

Not only do the National Committees raise funds for UNICEF, they also advocate for the organization in the industrialized world and serve as a sort of litmus test of popular support for UNICEF.

And without that support underpinning UNICEF, many a donor government might not be so generous with its contributions.

Which would mean less money to help us kids!

Today there are Committees in:

Andorra Austria Australia

Belgium Bulgaria **Canada**

Czech Republic Denmark Estonia

Finland **France** Germany Greece

Hong Kong Hungary

Ireland Israel Italy

Japan Latvia **Lithuania** Luxembourg

Netherlands **New Zealand** Norway

Poland Portugal **Republic of Korea**

Romania San Marino

Slovak Republic **Slovenia** Spain

Sweden Switzerland

Turkey United Kingdom **USA**

If any are missing, you put them down.

41

In 1964, the National Committees got an additional boost. That was the year it was decided that they could 'adopt' projects and earmark funds for them. Now they wouldn't have to rely on disasters to mobilize public generosity for children.

The National Committees have helped organize more than 200,000 volunteers on behalf of children.

The unsung heroes include:

Belgian Committee for UNICEF

The schoolchildren of Belgium who have raised tens of thousands of dollars to provide clean water to the children of Bolivia.

Irish truck driver **Christopher Groome,** who, during the African famine of the 1980s, organized a 43-truck convoy that traveled across the Emerald Isle, raising almost $13,000 for kids.

Frank Fennell

And French butcher **Claude Perret,** who sells 10,000 UNICEF greeting cards a year in his small shop in Paris.

1965 was a tumultuous year for UNICEF.

Henry Labouisse became UNICEF's second Executive Director in June after Maurice Pate died, of a heart attack.

An American, Labouisse had headed the UN Relief and Works Administration in the Middle East, which cared for nearly a million Palestinian refugees following the upheaval associated with the creation of Israel.

1965 was also the year UNICEF won the Nobel Prize for Peace. On December 10 in Oslo, Norway, Labouisse accepted the prize.

To me the most important meaning of this award is the solemn recognition that the welfare of today's children is inseparably linked with the peace of tomorrow's world. Their suffering and privations do not ennoble; they frustrate and embitter. The longer the world tolerates the slow war and attrition which poverty and ignorance wage...against 800 million children, the more likely it becomes that our hope for lasting peace will be the ultimate casualty.

UNICEF/1626

FAMILY PLANNING

Family planning was to become the most controversial aspect of the Labouisse years. By the 1960s, it was becoming clear that population rates were growing at unprecedented levels — the world's population would likely double in the next 20 to 30 years.

In 1966, Labouisse proposed to the Executive Board that UNICEF help governments already focusing on family planning to expand their mother and child services, expanding family planning elements of the program in the process. No contraceptives would be provided — just the usual UNICEF combo of training stipends and teaching aids. But even this modest plan provoked bitter debate.

Some countries were shocked by what they regarded as the proposal's implicit endorsement of contraception, and even threatened to cut their UNICEF funding. At the end of the debate, the issue was unresolved.

One year later, the World Health Organization stepped in. And following WHO directives, UNICEF was soon able to include family planning services as part of its regular health care programs in a number of countries. The UN Fund for Population Activities (now called the United Nations Population Fund) was created in 1970 to help deal with the controversial issue.

EMERGENCIES

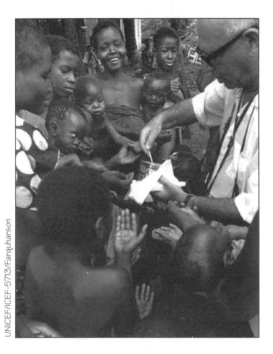

UNICEF/ICEF-5713/Farquharson

The first major crisis of Labouisse's term was the 1967 Nigerian civil war. UNICEF, because of its mandate to help children regardless of political considerations, was the only organization in a position to assist starving children in the blockaded, disputed Biafra area. During the three-year crisis, UNICEF was able to help children on both sides of the conflict.

During the late 1960s, there was continued debate about UNICEF's proper degree of involvement in disaster relief. In the era of development, UNICEF wanted to move beyond its role as chief Band-Aid supplier to the world.

We dropped the word emergency from UNICEF's name in 1953, remember?

In addition to the Nigerian civil war, UNICEF had spent countless resources to help bring relief to victims of an earthquake in Morocco and a famine in India — just in the 1960s. Despite the best intentions to work on long-term development, disasters demanded immediate response.

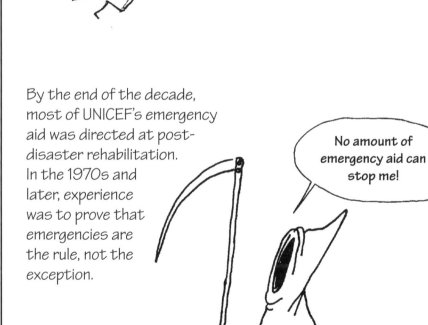

We don't have time to analyze the future! Kids need our help now!

By the end of the decade, most of UNICEF's emergency aid was directed at post-disaster rehabilitation. In the 1970s and later, experience was to prove that emergencies are the rule, not the exception.

No amount of emergency aid can stop me!

1970s

A child emergency should have been declared years ago!

A sudden world food shortage and a rise in the price of oil and fertilizer forced UNICEF to declare a **CHILD EMERGENCY** in the early 1970s. Perhaps 70 million children were suffering from some kind of nutritional deficiency. At least 10 million were close to starvation.

Many children were simply not getting enough to eat. For many others, the problem was a diet based on one kind of food, so they were lacking certain micronutrients, essential ingredients that everybody needs in their diet. Tiny amounts will do — that's where 'micro' comes in. Without them, the body can't develop properly. Iodine is a good illustration.

Iodine deficiency disorders

can cause a variety of handicaps, reduced intelligence, even cretinism.

I'll take this with a grain of salt.

Sometimes it causes a goiter — a large swelling on the neck due to an enlarged thyroid gland. And all that's needed to prevent iodine deficiency is adding iodine to salt.

There are two other major micronutrient deficiencies...

Lack of vitamin A

leads to night blindness and sometimes even total loss of vision. It also makes children more likely to die when they're sick, especially from measles or diarrhea. For want of four cents worth of vitamin A per day or a diet including yellow or green leafy vegetables, millions of children have endured blindness.

MINISTER OF HEALTH

Iron-deficiency anemia

afflicts perhaps half of all pregnant women in the developing world, causing exhaustion and poor health. Iron-deficient women are more likely to die in childbirth. Their babies often begin their lives underweight. Supplemental iron tablets costing one fifth of one cent per day are all that's needed to defeat iron-deficiency anemia.

In the 1970s, UNICEF worked hard to fuse adequate nutrition with a broader definition of health care.

But nutrition was far from the only problem to draw attention in the 1970s.

Some educators were beginning to diagnose a **world education crisis.** Certainly the economic crisis of the time was keeping many governments from maintaining, let alone expanding, their school systems. And several hundred million children weren't even in school.

Can you spell crisis?

In the 1970s, UNICEF began turning its attention to **non-formal education:** education outside the classroom.

It was aimed at working kids, adults who missed out on school when they were young — anybody who couldn't attend a regular school. With UNICEF's help, youth clubs, radio stations, women's groups, cooperative work and social groups, community newspapers and other organizations began teaching basic skills.

Non-formal? Does that mean no tuxedos in the classroom?

The idea was that every person needs a 'minimum package' of attitudes, skills and knowledge—a positive outlook, basic literacy and numeracy, understanding of the local environment, and the skills to raise a family, earn a living and take part in society.

Non-formal education was supposed to supplement, not replace, formal schools.

Some people saw it as second-class schooling, but eventually it came to have its own place in the education system.

And then there was health care.

Since the 1950s, UNICEF had helped to train thousands of midwives and pediatric personnel; it had equipped countless mother/child and maternity clinics too. But not enough of such services had reached the millions who lived in remote rural areas.

I'm afraid I'm going to have to remove your wallet.

Indeed, much of government health spending continued to be on expensive urban hospitals, not low-cost health clinics in the countryside. Sometimes the majority of the people had nowhere to turn for medical care.

In 1970, two Indian doctors started a new kind of health care in the state of Maharashtra, India. It would revolutionize health care in the developing world, for they decided what people needed were **COMMUNITY-BASED** health care workers.

Take two aspirin and call me in the morning.

अच्छा *

*Okay

The health workers were middle-aged women and respected members of the community. They held village meetings on nutrition, health and family planning. Each one also had a kit that included basic drugs.

UNICEF had long known that only when a community enthusiastically adopts an initiative as its own will it really work. Community-based health care workers seemed like a stroke of genius.

In the mid-1970s, the World Health Organization gave its blessing to such programs. Community-based health care soon dethroned the medical establishment as the official and only provider of health services.

INTERNATIONAL YEAR OF THE CHILD

1979, the 20th anniversary of the Declaration of the Rights of the Child, was designated INTERNATIONAL YEAR OF THE CHILD. That January, UN Headquarters in New York was rocked like never before. This time it wasn't controversy but rock and roll. The gala concert in celebration of the year was telecast to 60 countries and seen by 60 million people. The subsequent album raised $4 million for UNICEF.

UNICEF itself received a tremendous boost from the exposure the International Year of the Child gave to its work. Income from private contributions rose to $50 million, double that of the previous year.

During the year, people began to advocate for child rights. Many countries undertook national diagnoses of their children's situations, some for the first time.

But more importantly, kids benefited, particularly street children and disabled children.

Indeed, the plight of the world's estimated 70 million street children received so much attention that UNICEF was able to assist in efforts to reunite these children with their families.

UNICEF also commissioned a study on children's disabilities in developing countries.

UNICEF began supporting creative programs around the world, especially those trying to keep these kids with their families and in their communities.

CAMBODIA

Among the most moving of UNICEF's initiatives in the 1970s was its relief effort in Cambodia (then known as Kampuchea).

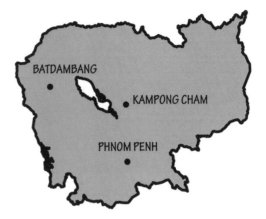

The country had been devastated by a terrible civil war and subsequent cruel dictatorship by the Khmer Rouge under Pol Pot. In 1979, the Vietnamese invaded and overthrew the Khmer Rouge, who retreated to the country's northwest and continued fighting. People trapped by the continuing warfare began to flee across the Thai border or take refuge in camps along the border, which brought fears of impending famine.

In the Kampuchean capital, Phnom Penh, UNICEF led relief operations, providing the necessary umbrella for assistance from other UN agencies and the International Committee of the Red Cross. As in Nigeria a decade before, UNICEF, with its non-political mandate, was one of the few agencies able to play such a role. The UNICEF-led Cambodian operation became the largest and most complex operation of its kind ever mounted.

Remember what Eglantyne Jebb* said: **"I have no enemies under the age of 11!"**

* Founder of Save the Children

The work was far from easy — operationally, diplomatically and financially. Logistical problems were so overwhelming that much of the assistance was slow to reach its destination. Still, by 1981, $634 million in assistance had been delivered inside the country and in refugee camps in Thailand and Viet Nam, and the famine crisis was over.

1980s

The new decade was ushered in with a new Executive Director for UNICEF.

Henry Labouisse had retired after 14 years of service. **James P. Grant**, former head of the US-based Overseas Development Council, had come aboard.

Grant was very concerned about the 'silent emergency' that was killing about 15 million children every year. By 1982 he had launched the **Child Survival and Development Revolution.** The 'revolution' was based on four simple and low-cost techniques that had already proved their weight in gold: the GOBI techniques, they came to be called.

rowth monitoring

ral rehydration
therapy

reastfeeding

mmunization

GROWTH
MONITORING

The problem of malnutrition is often a sneaky, invisible one. Most malnourished kids — 99 per cent, in fact — aren't starving. They are simply underweight, which diminishes their strength and energy. Chances are, though, that lack of proper nutrients and micronutrients will impede their development and make them more susceptible to disease.

But how's a mother to know if her child is malnourished? Growth monitoring! A child is weighed each month, and the results are plotted on a chart. Food supplements can then be distributed as needed.

ORT

Diarrhea is second only to pneumonia as a child killer. But, diarrhea doesn't kill outright. It's the dehydration it brings — the sudden loss of bodily fluid — that's so deadly. Oral rehydration therapy, or ORT, can change all that. ORT is actually a long name for a very simple cure.

Add sugar to a drink of salt and water.

BREASTFEEDING

Research proves that mother's milk has remarkable health and nutritional properties. But, in many parts of the world, bottle-feeding is unfortunately seen as the 'modern' way to feed little ones.

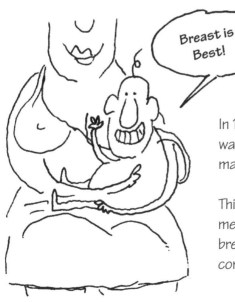

Breast is Best!

In 1981, an International Code was passed to limit the marketing of infant formula.

This was just one among many measures needed if breastfeeding was to make a comeback.

IMMUNIZATION

Six widespread communicable diseases:

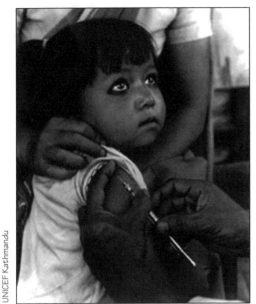

Diphtheria

Pertussis (known as Whooping Cough)

Tetanus

Measles

Polio

Tuberculosis

together kill millions of children a year for want of a 'jab' of immunization.

While none of these four measures was new, packaging them together and trying to implement them as a whole was. The idea was that, together, the effects of each measure would be amplified.

Using the GOBI strategy, Grant set a goal for the year 2000: reducing by half the estimated 15 million annual deaths of children under the age of five.

Grant also decided to publish an annual report on *The State of the World's Children*. The publication, launched in 1980, soon became his major advocacy platform.

But as to whether the Child Survival and Development Revolution would succeed — nobody would be more important than mothers.

After all, it was they who would decide whether to breastfeed or immunize or weigh their children.

As usual, the responsibility falls on us women.

In fact, it's the education of women, more than any other variable, that influences children's health. Kids born to mothers with no education are twice as likely to die in infancy as those born to mothers with as little as four years of schooling.

A woman's work is never done!

Grant's 'revolution' for children therefore included specific programs and goals for female education as well.

By 1985, the revolution was under way.

In Sri Lanka, a mass media campaign to promote breastfeeding coupled with a ban on advertising of infant formula helped increase breastfeeding in urban areas by 70 percent.

In Thailand, the number of growth charts in use quintupled to 2.5 million in just three years.

In Egypt, a national program was launched to halve the number of deaths from diarrhea by promoting ORT.

In Colombia, a massive vaccination crusade was so successful that 800,000 children were reached, raising the immunization rate to more than 75 percent.

In fact, there were so many vaccination campaigns in so many countries that demand for vaccines was running three times higher than just a decade earlier. UNICEF estimates that the lives of 1 million children were saved as a result.

No pain, no gain.

ow!

On October 24, 1985, during the UN's 40th anniversary celebrations, the General Assembly unanimously endorsed the goal of universal child immunization by 1990. By that year, 66 developing countries had achieved the 80 percent immunization target, preventing 3 million deaths a year.

The immunizaton drive even stopped a war in one country— if only for a few days.

Santa Ana

San Salvador

San Miguel

El Salvador

El Salvador was torn apart by civil war in the 1980s. But in the spring of 1985, a three-day vaccination ceasefire was arranged by UNICEF, the Government and the Catholic Church. Within 72 hours, 60 percent of all Salvadoran children had been immunized. (This approach was so successful, it was adopted in other countries — but more on that later.)

Shot Spot

There were other important ways UNICEF tried to help kids during the 1980s. For instance, through advocacy for

'adjustment with a human face'.

A number of developing countries, most of them in Africa and many of them under pressure from international lending institutions, took dramatic steps to reduce their national debts. Too often this meant cutting essential government services to the poor!

UNICEF spent much of the 1980s trying to convince key decision makers to safeguard the most vulnerable, especially children, during times of adjustment and austerity.

And not only that. UNICEF argued that policy makers rarely understood the contribution some of those vulnerable groups make to a nation's economic development. Throughout most of Africa, for instance, women grow most of the food consumed locally. In more than one instance, their work has helped nations out of nasty food shortages.

For a government to invest in its people, then, is not only kind but smart.

One initiative intended to improve the health of Africans in the 1980s was...

THE BAMAKO INITIATIVE.

The initiative, named after the capital of Mali, where a health care conference was held in 1988, sought to radically redefine the health care systems of the continent.

How so?

Participants reasoned that many of the poorest people in Africa had no access to health care. Those who did were spending 5-10 percent of their incomes on medical services. They often had to rely on quacks and unscrupulous drug peddlers to buy much-needed medications.

OK, so what do you **do** about it?

Our health center doesn't even have medicine!

Perhaps the local communities themselves should manage and finance their own health services. Maybe they could take some of the money being wasted on ineffective or expensive medicines and pool it to buy generic drugs in mass quantities at a much lower price through local health committees.

Exactly! And more sophisticated drugs would be available at the district level. The idea is for community-managed health care to become primarily self-financing.

It's too early to know if community-financed health care will work. But so far the results have been encouraging.

The very end of the 1980s brought some extraordinary news for the world's children.

CONVENTION ON THE RIGHTS OF THE CHILD

For some years several governments and NGOs had been pushing for a new treaty on children's rights. UNICEF envisioned it as the clearest expression of what the international community would promise its children. And unlike the 1959 Declaration of the Rights of the Child, this treaty was to be legally binding. The Convention on the Rights of the Child, it would be called, for conventions, unlike declarations, are indeed legally binding.

You PROMISE?

CONVENTION ON THE RIGHTS OF THE CHILD

And just what **would** the convention pledge?

Well, among other things: an inherent right to life . . . a right to a name and nationality and education . . . and special care for disabled children, . . . and of course protection from abuse and neglect and sexual exploitation and torture . . . access to information and the right to enjoy one's culture . . . and a good standard of living . . . and protection for kids without families . . . and prevention of kidnapping . . .

No — there's more ...

Freedom of association . . . the right to play, to see one's parents . . . and protection from drugs and libel . . . and from being sold or abducted or recruited into armed forces . . . and freedom of thought and religion . . . and adoption only when necessary . . . and a right to justice . . . and rights for child victims . . . and the right to protection from maltreatment by caregivers . . . and the right to . . .

And on November 20, 1989, the Convention on the Rights of the Child was adopted by the General Assembly. Two months later, it was opened for signature at UN Headquarters. That very day, 61 countries signed. No other human rights treaty had ever gathered such support so quickly.

As of January 1996, all but six countries of the world had ratified it.

Needless to say, a universally accepted code for the treatment of children would be a tremendous step forward. It would:

Provide an unchallenged platform for advocacy and action on behalf of kids everywhere!!

And it would also prepare the way for the next and clearly more difficult step—

Moving from universal acceptance

to universal observance.

1990s

The decade began with a bang!

On September 30, 1990, 71 Presidents and Prime Ministers came to New York to attend the first-ever **World Summit for Children**. Never before had so many world leaders gathered together.

But what did it **do?**

In a word — lots! To begin with, for 24 hours the needs of children claimed the exclusive attention of many of the world's most important decision makers.

Cheese!

The meeting, among other things, established the principle of **"first call for children,"** meaning that children should get priority attention in bad times and good. Those attending the Summit agreed that certain goals must be achieved by the year 2000.

1. **Reduction of Childhood Deaths by One Third.**
About 14 million kids were dying every year from easily preventable diseases.

2. **Reduction by Half of Maternal Deaths.**
Around 500,000 women were dying every year because something went wrong with pregnancy or childbirth.

3. **Reduction by Half of Malnutrition.**
One out of three children in the developing world was being prevented from reaching his or her full potential by persistent malnutrition.

4. **Universal Access to Safe Water and Clean Sanitation,** to prevent water-borne diseases such as diarrhea, which was causing so much sickness and death.

5. **Universal Access to Basic Education,** with at least 80 percent of children finishing primary school. Only half of all kids in developing countries were completing even four years of primary school. Girls were about half as likely as boys to have stayed in school long enough to become literate.

6. **Reduction by Half of Adult Illiteracy,** with special attention on encouraging female literacy. Two thirds of the over 900 million adults who couldn't read and write were women!

7. **Protection of Children in Especially Difficult Circumstances, particularly those in Armed Conflict.** More than 100 million children were living in war zones.

Later, a number of 'mid-decade goals', to be achieved by 1995, were established to make sure countries stayed on track.

The problem, as usual, was money. And what about dreaming beyond the goals? It was estimated that to end preventable childhood death and malnutrition and to ensure the world's children 'normal development', an additional **$25 billion** per year would have to be spent for at least the rest of the decade.

So, what kind of money are we talking?

Why, think of all the bombs that money would buy!

So much money, compared to UNICEF's resources! And yet the world spends $20 billion on military expenditures about every 10 days.

Five Years Later...

...there was good news — at least concerning the goals.

By the end of 1995, the majority of developing nations — more than 100 countries, with 90 percent of the world's children — had achieved the majority of those 'mid-decade' goals.

Malnutrition had been reduced, immunization levels maintained or increased. In fact, immunization campaigns have been so successful that 145 countries became polio free by late 1995, and deaths from measles had fallen dramatically as well. Also...

Micronutrient disorders, especially iodine and vitamin A deficiencies, were being overcome. The use of oral rehydration therapy was rising dramatically. Breastfeeding was up...

However, 12.8 million children were still dying every year, most of them from easily preventable diseases. But just a few years ago that figure was 15 million. Progress has been made against the 'silent emergency'.

More and more kids are being threatened by very loud emergencies—like wars and natural disasters .

In the good old days, wars were fought between armies. But things have changed. Today, wars kill and maim far more civilians, mainly children and women, than soldiers. In the past decade alone, an estimated 2 million children have been killed in armed conflict; 4 million to 5 million disabled; 12 million left homeless.

Q:

Why *do so many* combatants commit atrocities?

WAR

PEACE

A:

Er, to give the children a better future?

And then there are the millions of children who have been traumatized, such as by seeing people killed or being forced to watch or even participate in the torture of family members or neighbors. Such scars run deep.

Indeed, it's difficult even to estimate how many children are suffering from post-traumatic stress disorders, a chilling new term in the international lexicon. Often the clinic where a child might have received help has been destroyed. So too have schools and crops.

No, I don't think I want to play war today...

There's even more. Many children have been recruited into armies, given drugs, then weapons, and systematically desensitized to the pain suffered by others, before being forced into combat.

And what about the **landmine** casualties? Hundreds of thousands more people have been crippled and killed by landmines. In many areas of the world, children constitute about half the victims of mines. Countless others face worsening poverty and hunger, thanks to mines having been sown into agricultural fields.

No one knows how many mines have been placed where. But in 1995 the UN put the figure at **more than 100 million in 64 countries.**

→ Iran has 16 million landmines.

→ Angola has 15 million — more mines than people.

→ Afghanistan's war has left 10 million uncleared mines.

→ Cambodia has 10 million.

→ Bosnia and Herzegovina has 3 million.

The UN is involved in mine-clearing operations, but the job is slow and expensive. It may cost as little as $3 to buy one, but the price for locating and de-activating that mine is $300-$1,000.

UNICEF and others have called for a worldwide ban on the production, use, stockpiling, sale and export of mines. But landmine production is thought to be a $100 million-per-year industry — it is unlikely to shut itself down for magnanimous reasons!

UNICEF/ICEF/ 6671/Danois

There's one hopeful sign, though: 30 countries have announced full or partial moratoriums on landmine exports as of the end of 1995.

Those kids are playing with detonated rockets!

Even when the international community takes actions designed to
punish those responsible for waging war on innocents, those actions
can end up hurting children. Take

ECONOMIC SANCTIONS,
for instance.

They are very much a double-
edged sword. Often the heaviest
consequences fall on those who
are most innocent and
vulnerable.

Scarcity and rising prices make the poor that much more desperate, while bringing only minor inconveniences to the wealthy and powerful.

As important as such sanctions can be politically, UNICEF believes it is imperative to think through, in advance, their likely impact and develop ways to help their unintended victims, all too often children.

Isn't there anything we can do to protect children from the horrors of the adult world?

 **YES!**

Such as?

1. There's the **Convention on the Rights of the Child,** for instance. After all, it includes specific provisions for the protection of children in areas of armed conflict. But it needs to be enforced.

2. And remember the immunization program arranged during the height of the civil war in El Salvador? Similar **'Days of Tranquility'** have been used to bring humanitarian assistance to other countries undergoing conflict, including Iraq, Lebanon, Sudan, Uganda and the former Yugoslavia.

3. Dozens of **non-governmental organizations, NGOs** as they're often called, are working tirelessly to help children affected by war.

4. But whatever progress is being made, it can only be maintained by loud and insistent **public demand for action.** So there really is something you can do. Speak up! Write letters! Join groups! Or start your own! Everybody needs to be mobilized in the struggle for children's rights.

Everybody
needs to get involved: parents and policy makers, plumbers and doctors, computer programmers and nurses, bureaucrats and journalists, presidents and kids.

Social development won't happen without public action, no matter how worthy the cause.

What does UNICEF do to get the public involved? Write books, I suppose.

Expert

Well, yes, but books and publications are only one aspect of UNICEF's information and advocacy work.

The State of the World's Children

Children Just Like Me

I Dream of Peace

The Progress of Nations

UNICEF is also involved in mass communication projects that seek to change the way we see and treat children. Take, for instance, the **Meena** project, which combines animated films, comic books and radio programs. Thus far Meena has been produced in 18 languages.

Meena isn't just a cartoon character, she is a role model for girls and boys...

...especially in South Asia, where girls face so much discrimination.

Using cartoons to educate?! It CAN'T be done!

Present book excepted, of course.

EXPERT

Like other, more traditional UNICEF communication efforts, Meena aims to develop a groundswell of popular support to change attitudes and behaviors — among people and societies. Also in typical UNICEF style, the project tries to create alliances, such as with NGOs, to help promote rights. It has been seen by millions of people, female and male, young and old.

It's important to remember it was mobilization of ordinary people that helped defeat slavery and colonialism. It will be through our efforts that modern-day discrimination is ended, too!

Golly, I help do all that?

UH HUH!

✳ ✳ ✳ ✳ ✳ ✳ ✳

In 1995, **Carol Bellamy** became the first woman to serve as UNICEF's Executive Director. Bellamy previously had been head of the US Peace Corps, as well as a New York State Senator and New York City Council President.

She replaced James Grant, who had died after a long battle with cancer.

As UNICEF approached its 50th anniversary year, Ms. Bellamy used **_The State of the World's Children 1996_** to announce UNICEF's anti-war agenda.

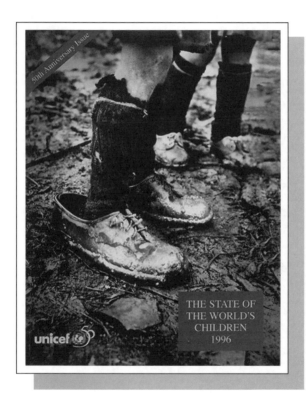

It recognizes the sad symmetry that, 50 years after UNICEF was born of war in 1946, millions of children around the world are still suffering from the consequences of conflict between and within countries.

The 10-point agenda, whose guiding force is the **Convention on the Rights of the Child,** calls for raising the minimum age of military recruitment from 15, as currently set out in the Convention, to 18 years and for passage of an international law banning landmines.

The anti-war agenda also calls for schools to teach about peace and tolerance, and for a 'child impact assessment' of economic sanctions *before* they are applied.

Through these and other points of the agenda, UNICEF calls on the world to insist that warring parties be obliged to apply the child protections provided by the Convention on the Rights of the Child.

With almost every country in the world having ratified the Convention, it is now a powerful tool for citizens, non-governmental organizations and agencies such as UNICEF to demand enforcement of child rights.

2000?

Well, as we face the new millenium there's good news and bad news.

The biggest threat to the world's poorest billion people is no one thing — not war, not even the 'silent emergency' alone. Rather, it's the very sinister interaction of poverty, population growth and environmental degradation.

A vicious cycle is formed: poverty increases population growth, which leads to environmental stress, which in turn worsens poverty.

Take for instance  poverty

Today 1.3 billion people, or more than one fifth of the world's population, live in absolute poverty.

Poverty causes high death rates, which in turn lead couples to have more children to ensure that some will survive. Poor parents not only love their children, they need them — both to make ends meet and as old-age security.

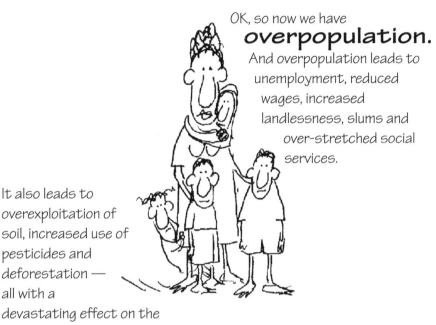

OK, so now we have **overpopulation.** And overpopulation leads to unemployment, reduced wages, increased landlessness, slums and over-stretched social services.

It also leads to overexploitation of soil, increased use of pesticides and deforestation — all with a devastating effect on the **environment.**

While poverty is the root cause of the population and environmental crisis in the developing world, poverty also presents the easiest point at which to break the cycle.

What is needed is an international effort to combat world poverty.

Save the Humans

Which of course brings us back to the goals that the World Summit for Children laid out to be achieved by the year 2000.

The world needs to make four basic investments. They would aim to:

1. Prevent common diseases and disabilities and steeply reduce malnutrition.

that's doable

2. Make sure all children complete primary school.

that's doable

ABC

3. Improve the lives of poor women — their health, education, status, rights and opportunities.

4. Make family planning information and services available to all who need them.

It's an investment that UNICEF's new
Executive Director believes would
bring a big return:

> I dream of the
> day when the world's
> children will no longer
> need UNICEF.

**That will happen only when the needs of all the world's
children are fulfilled — when they go to sleep each night
well-fed, healthy, confident of their safety in their homes
and communities, and full of the joy of youth.**

And it won't happen unless we MAKE it happen. The children of the
world are waiting.

> GO FOR IT!

Christian Clark won two Emmy awards as a writer for Sesame Street. His cartoons have appeared in publications including *Punch* magazine, *The Washington Post* and India's *The Illustrated Weekly*. He has been a UNICEF Information Officer in Zaire and Somalia and is currently with UNICEF's office in Nepal.

The United Nations Children's Fund works with governments in 144 countries to help meet the essential needs of children. It is funded entirely by voluntary contributions from governments and individuals.

Index

Thailand, 69
trachoma, 19
tuberculosis, 19

 United Nations Relief and
Works Administration, 44
Ustinov, Peter, 39

vaccines, 19, 66, 69-71
vitamin A deficiency disorders, 51, 85

Ullmann, Liv, 38
UNICEF (United Nations
Childrens Fund):
    creation and mandate of,
    1-2, 5, 9
    debate about future of,
    8-12
    emblem of, 29
    Executive Director and
    Board, 5
    funding of, 5, 31-43
    greeting cards, 31-34
    National Committees,
    40-42
    Nobel Prize for Peace
    award to, 45
    warehouse in Copenhagen,
    22
United Kingdom, 6
United Nations Bureau of
Social Affairs, 9
United Nations Population
Fund, 47
United Nations Relief and
Rehabilitation Organization,
2

war emergencies, UNICEF
relief work, 2
women's rights, 68, 105
World Health Organization, 9,
14-16, 47, 56
World Summit for Children,
81-82
World War II, 2

Yaws, 15-17

uni

cef

BAMAKO
FOR
BEGINNERS

IF YOU LIKED UNICEF...

THE U.N. FOR BEGINNERS

BY IAN WILLIAMS

The U.N. for Beginners by Ian Williams

For half a century, most people have agreed on the importance of the United Nations—but most of us have no idea how the bloody thing works! With wit and irony, *The U.N. for Beginners* takes a critcally supportive look at the U.N. and its components, cutting through the red tape to show the gaps between dreams and reality. This overview of the world's most famous organization is accessible to beginners and refreshing for the more experienced.

Paper, $11.00 ($15.95 Cnd.), ISBN 0-86316-185-5

coming soon!

I-Ching for Beginners
By Brendan Toropov   Illustrated by John Kane

For 3,000 years, the I-Ching, or Book of Changes, has been considered one of the most important books of philosophy and divination. The author uses Jung's theory of "synchronicity" to help Westerners undertand the logic behind the ancient Chinese art of divination. The book is so well-conceived that any reader with three coins can use the book to answer virtually any question. Make no mistake: The I-Ching contains profound insights about the human condition, and (most pragmatic of all) simply works.

Paper $11.00 ($15.95 Cdn.) ISBN 0-86316-230-4

Eastern Europe for Beginners
By Beck, Mast, and Tapper

Bought a new map lately? It is probably out of date, especially in Eastern Europe, where borders have been changing faster than mapmaker can mapmake. Most of us can't keep up with the dizzying speed of events in the former Yugoslavia, the former Czechoslovakia, etc. If you're trying to sift through the layers of propaganda and misinformation, or if you're just trying to understand what you read in the newspapers, this is the book you need!

Paper $11.00 ($15.95 Cdn.) ISBN 0-86316-237-1

Chomsky For Beginners

By David Cogswell   Illustrated by Paul Gordon

The breadth of Chomsky's learning and influence is unparalleled in modern times: he has made great contributions to linguistics, philosophy, and politics. So why don't you know more about him?

Don't worry, you will after you read **Chomsky for Beginners**!

Paper $11.00 ($15.95 Cdn.) ISBN 0-86316-233-9

Race For Beginners

By S.E. Anderson

Everyone knows what "race" is, right? <u>Wrong!</u> Race and its deadly offshoot, racism, are both considerably different than you think. Author S.E. Anderson follows his groundbreaking **The Black Holocaust for Beginners** with this new volume which clarifies and enriches the earlier book.

Paper $11.00 ($15.95 Cdn.)
ISBN 0-86316-232-0

McLuhan For Beginners

By W. Terrence Gordon   Illustrated by Susan Willmarth

Marshall McLuhan, one of the most influential thinkers of the mid 20th century, pioneered the study of the Media and unified Art and Science. And who better to write his book than W. Terrence Gordon, McLuhan's official biographer!

Paper $11.00 ($15.95 Cdn.)
ISBN 0-86316-231-2

soon!

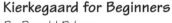

Kierkegaard for Beginners
By Donald Palmer

This illustrated book introduces the reader to one of the most amazing, difficult, and influential thinkers of the ninteenth century, Soren Kierkegaard. Kierkegaard's attack on social and religious conmplacency–along with his single-handed assault on traditional Western philosophy–generated a philosophical crisis that resulted in a radically new way of "doing philosophy."

Paper $11.00 ($15.95 Cdn.) ISBN 0-86316-192-8

Structuralism for Beginners
By Donald Palmer

This book is an illustrated tour through the mysterious landscape of structuralism and post-structuralism. The journey's starting point is the linguistic theory of Ferdinand de Saussure, then, jumping over the two world wars, it visits the key ideas of some of the big names in French thought between 1950 and 1980.

Paper $11.00 ($15.95 Cdn.)
ISBN 0-86316-193-6

Biology for Beginners
By Wilson McCord

This profusely illustrated book introduces the reader to biology–the study of life–in its natural / historical progression– that is, in the chronology in which the art and science of biology was discovered and pieced together throughout history.

Paper $11.00 ($15.95 Cdn.) ISBN 0-86316-194-4

HOW TO GET GREAT THINKERS TO COME TO YOUR HOME...

 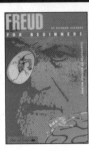  

To order any current titles of Writers and Readers **For Beginners**™ books, please fill out the coupon below and enclose a check made out to **Writers and Readers Publishing, Inc.** To order by phone (with Master Card or Visa), or to receive a <u>free catalog</u> of all our **For Beginners**™ books, please call (212) 982-3158.

Individual Order Form	(clip out or copy complete page)	
Book Title	**Quantity**	**Amount**
	Sub Total:	
N.Y. residents add 8 1/4% sales tax		
Shipping & Handling ($3.00 for the first book; $.60 for each additional book)		
	TOTAL	

Name _____

Address _____

City _____ State _____ Zip Code _____

Phone number (___) _____

MC / VISA (circle one)   Account # _____ Expires _____

Addiction & Recovery ($11.00)
African History ($9.95)
Arabs & Israel ($11.00)
Architecture ($11.00)
Babies ($9.95)
Biology ($11.00)
Black History ($9.95)
Black Holocaust ($11.00)
Black Panthers ($11.00)
Black Women ($9.95)
Brecht ($9.95)
Classical Music ($9.95)
Computers ($11.00)
DNA ($9.95)
Domestic Violence ($11.00)
Elvis ($6.95)
Erotica ($7.95)
Food ($7.95)
Foucault ($9.95)
Freud ($9.95)
Health Care ($9.95)
Heidegger ($9.95)
Hemingway ($9.95)
History of Clowns ($11.00)
Ireland ($9.95)
Islam ($9.95)
Jazz ($11.00)
Jewish Holocaust ($11.00)
J.F.K. ($9.95)
Judaism ($9.95)
Kierkegaard ($11.00)
Malcolm X ($9.95)
Mao ($9.95)
Martial Arts ($11.00)
Miles Davis ($9.00)
Nietzsche ($9.95)
Opera ($11.00)
Orwell ($4.95)
Pan-Africanism ($9.95)
Philosophy ($11.00)
Plato ($11.00)
Psychiatry ($9.95)
Rainforests ($7.95)
Sartre ($11.00)
Saussure ($11.00)
Sex ($9.95)
UNICEF ($11.00)
United Nations ($11.00)
World War II ($8.95)
Zen ($11.00)

Writers and Readers